WOULD YOU RATHER...

VISIT DISNEYLAND OR JURASSIC PARK?

...AND OTHER MAMMOTH QUESTIONS ABOUT PREHISTORIC ANIMALS

www.worldbook.com

WOULD YOU RATHER VISIT DISNEYLAND OR JURASSIC PARK?

It's fun to think about big questions and to ask yourself what you would do in strange situations. Here are a bunch of questions that World Book came up with, along with some advice from our editors. You don't have to arrive at the same answer as we did. What's important is that you exercise your imagination and critical thinking skills.

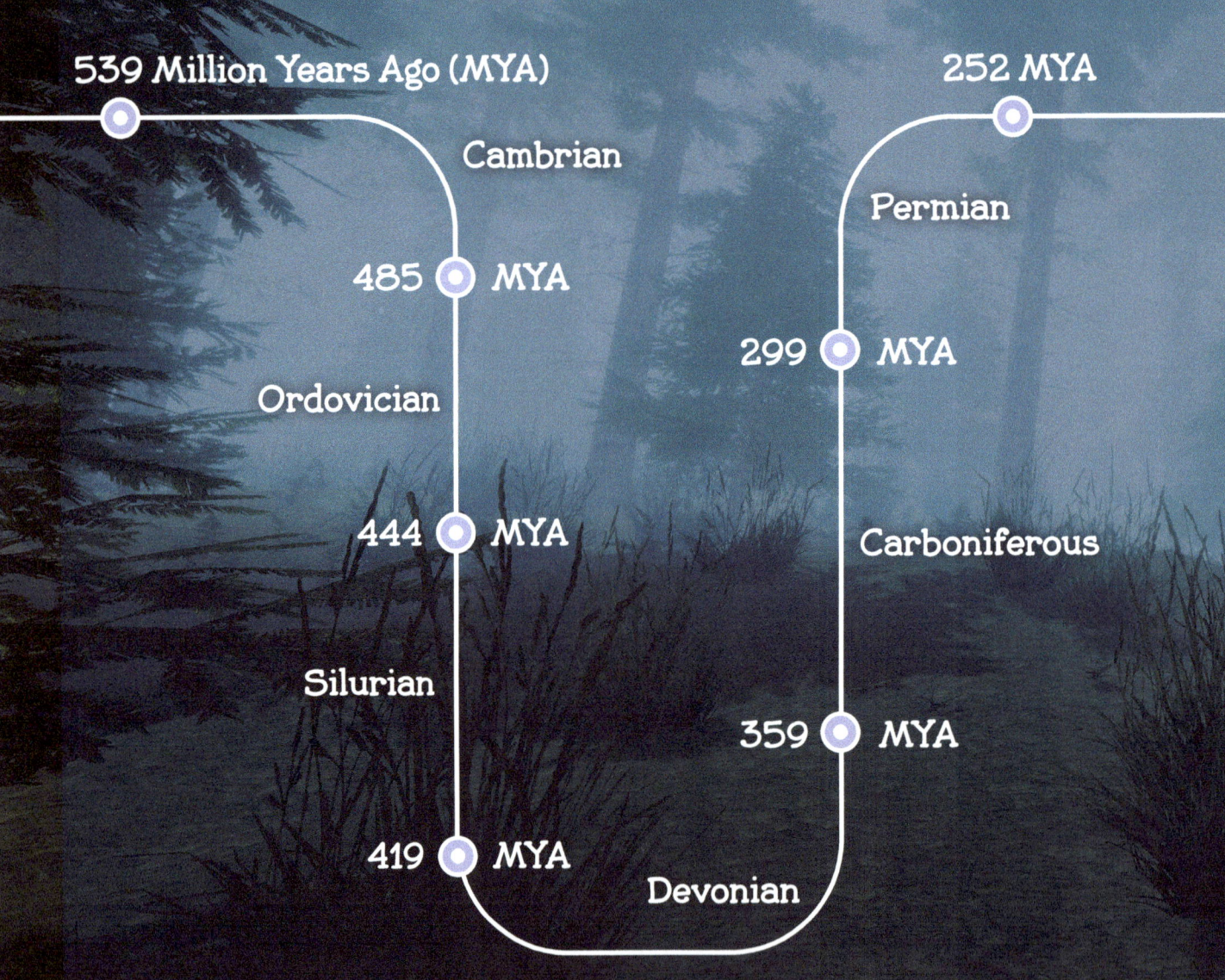

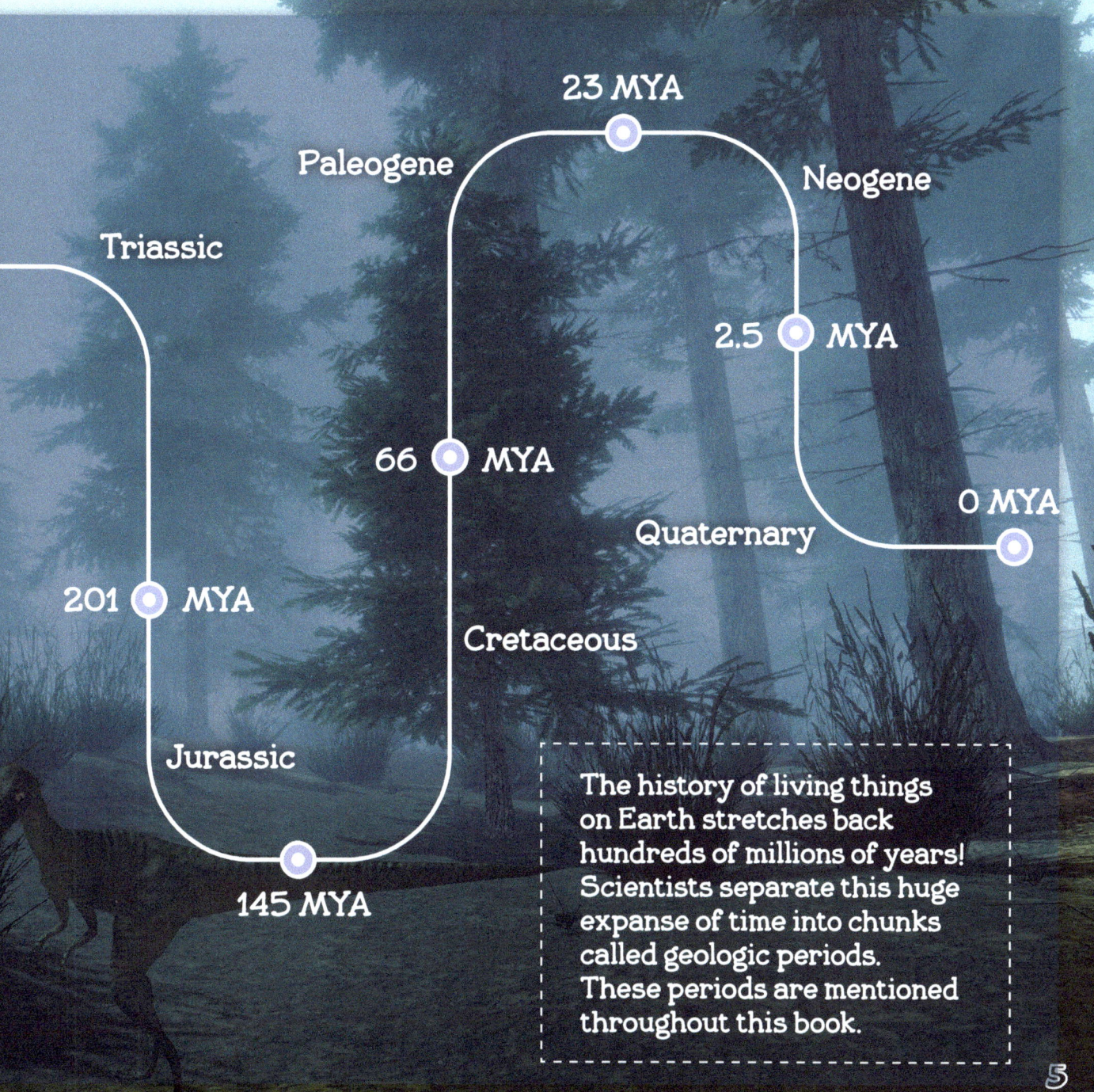

The history of living things on Earth stretches back hundreds of millions of years! Scientists separate this huge expanse of time into chunks called geologic periods. These periods are mentioned throughout this book.

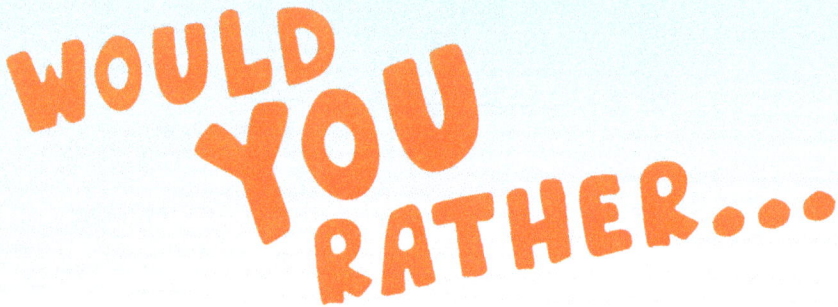

HAVE THE FIRST MAMMAL OR

THE FIRST DINOSAUR AS A PET?

Scientists don't agree on exactly when the first mammal appeared. But, it probably resembled a mouse or small weasel. An ordinary hamster cage might make the perfect palace for such a pint-sized pet.

The first dinosaur, on the other hand, was the 3-foot (1-meter) long *Eoraptor*. It lived in the middle Triassic Period. *Eoraptor* was a predator and would probably get into a lot of trouble.

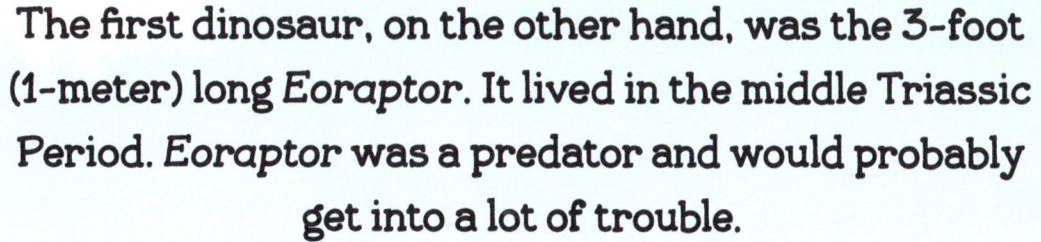

WHO WOULD WIN IN A FIGHT— TYRANNOSAURUS REX

OR SPINOSAURUS, THE LARGEST DINOSAUR PREDATOR KNOWN?

Spinosaurus was definitely larger. It reached 50 feet (15 meters) in length, compared to 40 feet (12 meters) for *Tyrannosaurus*. But don't give the trophy to *Spino* just yet! Fossils suggest *Spinosaurus* was at least partly *aquatic* (water-living), and its crocodilelike jaws were probably good for catching fish.

T. rex, on the other hand, had the jaws of a mega-predator, with teeth the size and shape of bananas for crushing through bone! Bet on *T. rex* in a fight.

WOULD YOU RATHER...

...HAVE A MAMMOTH-HAIR SWEATER OR AN ARCHAEOPTERYX-DOWN JACKET TO KEEP YOU WARM ON A COLD DAY?

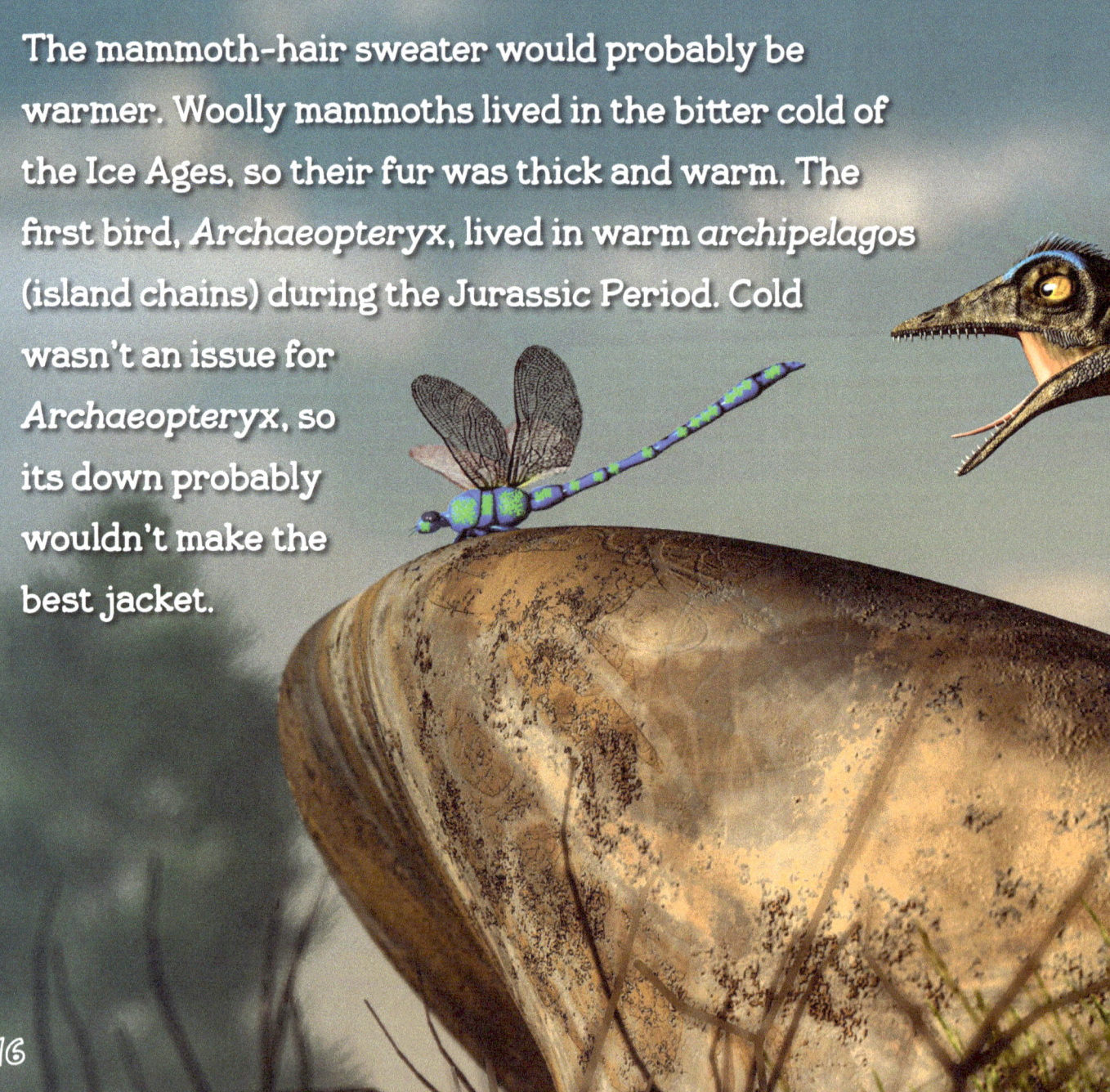

The mammoth-hair sweater would probably be warmer. Woolly mammoths lived in the bitter cold of the Ice Ages, so their fur was thick and warm. The first bird, *Archaeopteryx*, lived in warm *archipelagos* (island chains) during the Jurassic Period. Cold wasn't an issue for *Archaeopteryx*, so its down probably wouldn't make the best jacket.

The fictional Jurassic Park has an amazing collection of prehistoric animals. Perhaps the only thing more amazing is the park's disastrous safety record. Visitors seem likely as not to end up a dinosaur's lunch.

Disneyland would be a much safer vacation—so long as a rogue *Tyrannosaurus rex* doesn't accidentally get shipped to Southern California! (This actually happened in the movie *The Lost World: Jurassic Park*.)

WOULD YOU RATHER...

GET BITTEN BY THE TULLY MONSTER

The mysterious Tully monster lived during the late Carboniferous Period. It may have been an early fish or a mollusk, like a cuttlefish or clam.

WHO ARE YOU CALLING A MONSTER?

Whatever the case, it was a tiny monster, growing little more than 1 foot (33 centimeters) in length. It may look scary, but it couldn't do much damage with its tiny, hoselike mouth.

Sea scorpions (also known as eurypterids) actually couldn't sting you. But, you still wouldn't want to mess with one. They were fearsome lobsterlike predators that lived from the Ordovician Period to the Permian Period.

SOME GREW OVER 7 FEET (2 METERS) LONG!

WHICH IS CREEPIER—

THE LARGEST MILLIPEDE EVER OR THE LARGEST COCKROACH EVER?

The largest cockroaches that ever lived are alive today. Some rain forest cockroaches grow to about 5 inches (13 centimeters) long. That's pretty big, but it's nothing compared to the largest millipede ever.

The millipede *Arthropleura* lived from the early Carboniferous Period to the early Permian Period.

IT COULD GROW OVER 6 ½ FEET (2 METERS) LONG AND 20 INCHES (50 CENTIMETERS) WIDE. YIKES!

WOULD YOU RATHER...

HAVE THE BIGGEST SHELL OR THE STRONGEST JAWS?

30

Believe it or not, the animals with these features fought it out during the Neogene Period in northern South America.

Stupendemys was a river turtle with a shell measuring about 8 feet (2.4 meters) long. *Purussasaurus* was a *caiman* (a type of alligatorlike reptile) measuring over 40 feet (12 meters) long.

Purussaurus had a thick, squared-off jaw and ate whatever it pleased—such as this surprised Phoberomys.

THE JAWS HAVE IT!

WHO WOULD BE KING OF THE CAVE— THE CAVE LION OR THE CAVE BEAR?

The cave lion and the cave bear both roamed Europe during the last ice age. Neither spent more time in caves than do modern bears or lions. Scientists just call them "cave" animals because that's where their bones have been found.

Cave lions were about the same size as modern lions, weighing as much as 500 pounds (230 kilograms). There is evidence that they actually ate cave bear cubs. But a full-grown cave bear tipped the scales at 1,800 pounds (800 kilograms) or more.

A CAVE LION WOULD HAVE NO CHANCE AGAINST SUCH A TITAN.

WOULD YOU RATHER...

BE TRAPPED IN AMBER OR GET STUCK IN

THE LA BREA TAR PITS?

AMBER IS A HARD, YELLOWISH-BROWN FOSSILIZED RESIN THAT CAME FROM TREES.

Trees rarely release resin in large enough quantities to trap even small *vertebrates* (animals with backbones). So, if you're bigger than a bug, you're probably safe. The La Brea Tar Pits, on the other hand, became the oily graves of more than 1 million large prehistoric animals.

THERE'D BE NO ESCAPE!

WHICH CAME FIRST— THE CHICKEN OR THE EGG?

THIS ONE'S A NO-BRAINER: THE EGG.

The first birds arose from dinosaurs during the Jurassic Period, and the modern chicken came much later than that.

Dinosaurs had already been laying eggs for millions of years, and they weren't even the first in the egg-laying game.

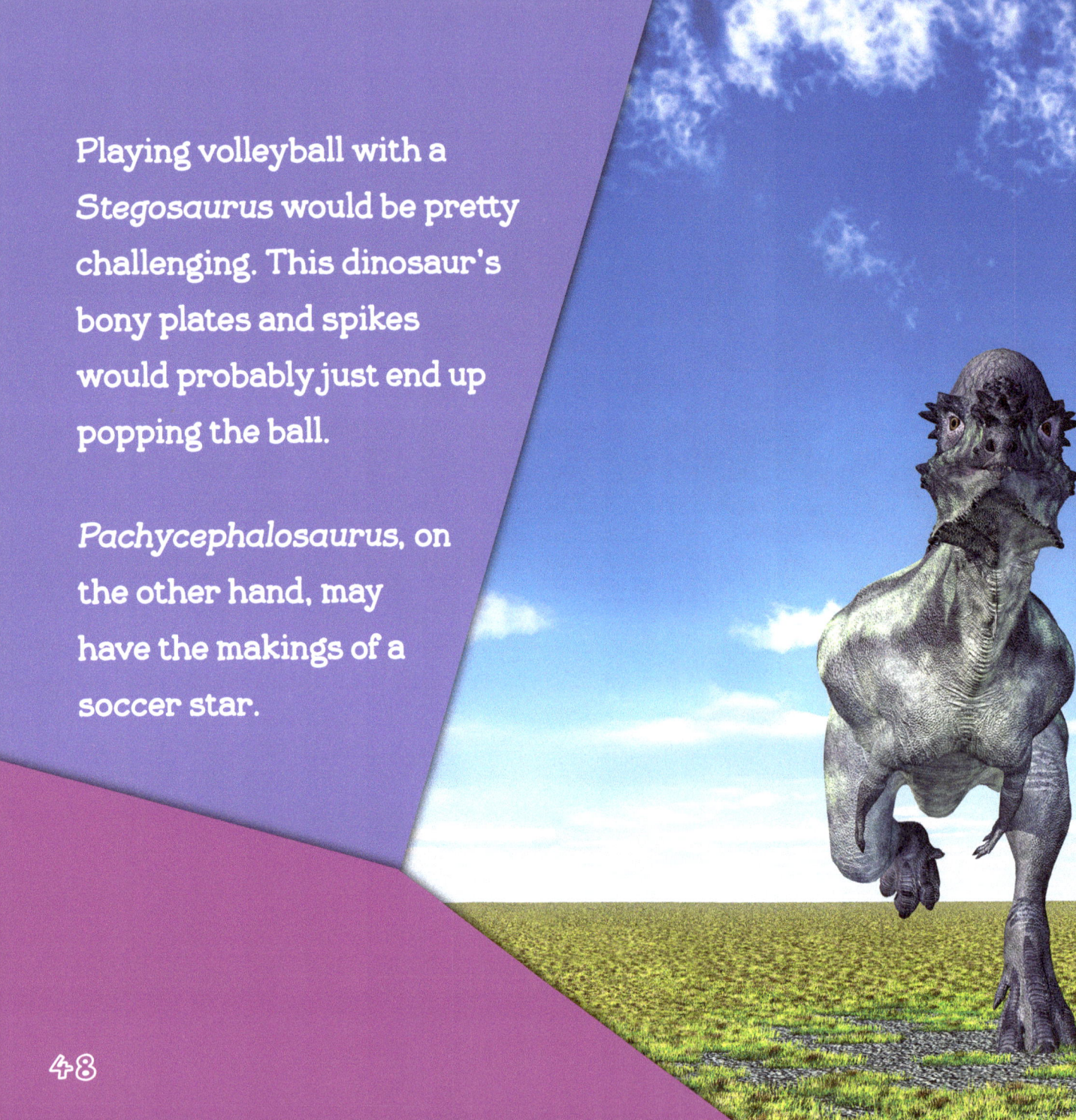

Playing volleyball with a *Stegosaurus* would be pretty challenging. This dinosaur's bony plates and spikes would probably just end up popping the ball.

Pachycephalosaurus, on the other hand, may have the makings of a soccer star.

...PARTY WITH AN ALLOSAURUS OR HANG OUT WITH THE DEMON DUCK OF DOOM?

The demon duck of doom sounds pretty frightening. That nickname was given to the huge, flightless bird *Bullockornis*. *Bullockornis* lived in what is now Australia during the Neogene Period. It stood about 8 feet (2.5 meters) tall. The "demon duck" name refers in part to its huge beak. But most scholars think *Bullockornis* was a plant-eater. *Bullockornis* would probably be better company than the dinosaur *Allosaurus*.

With this huge meat-eater, you'd probably end up on the menu.

WHO WOULD WIN IN

A MAMMOTH

A FIGHT BETWEEN AND A MASTODON?

If a mammoth is like the sibling of a modern elephant, a mastodon is like its second cousin. These beasts rubbed woolly shoulders during the Quaternary Period. They probably stayed out of each other's way for the most part. Mammoths ate grasses, while mastodons ate twigs and leaves.

BUT IN A TUSSLE, I'D GO WITH A MASTODON.

I'M NOT FEELING VERY STOCKY ANYMORE!

Both are about the same size. But, mastodons were stockier and had straighter tusks—which might be able to spear a foe. Some mastodon tusks stretched over 16 feet (5 meters) in length!

...enter a long-jump contest against a modern red kangaroo or the extinct giant kangaroo?

The giant kangaroo, *Procoptodon*, appeared 1 to 2 million years ago, during the Quaternary Period. Adults could weigh as much as 500 pounds (230 kilograms). That's about four times as much as a modern red kangaroo. But giant size doesn't necessarily equal giant leaps. Many scholars think *Procoptodon* was too heavy to hop very far, if at all. You would have a better chance against *Procoptodon* than against the red kangaroo, which can easily leap 25 feet (7.6 meters).

The Stone Age is a time when people used stone tools, rather than metal. It began about 3.3 million years ago and ended about 5,000 years ago, when people started using bronze. An ice age is any period in Earth's history when ice sheets covered vast regions of land. The most recent ice age ended about 11,500 years ago.

> I WISH I'D BEEN BORN IN THE BRONZE AGE!

THAT MEANS A FEW OF YOUR ANCESTORS LIVED IN THE STONE AGE AND AN ICE AGE AT THE SAME TIME!

Tools help make our lives easier. I'd rather have stone tools than no tools—with or without ice.

Would you rather...

Ride a Triceratops or a Pterosaur?

Pterosaurs are flying reptiles that lived alongside (but mostly above) dinosaurs in the Triassic, Jurassic, and Cretaceous periods. The largest, *Quetzalcoatlus*, had a wingspread approaching 40 feet (12 meters)! But even the Big Q probably couldn't get far with the added weight of a human rider.

The ground-pounding *Triceratops* was about 25 feet (7 ½ meters) long. It stood about 9 ½ feet (3 meters) tall at the hips and weighed about 8 tons (7 ½ metric tons)—big enough to carry the whole family!

...SHARE YOUR ROOM WITH A GROUND SLOTH OR A TREE SLOTH?

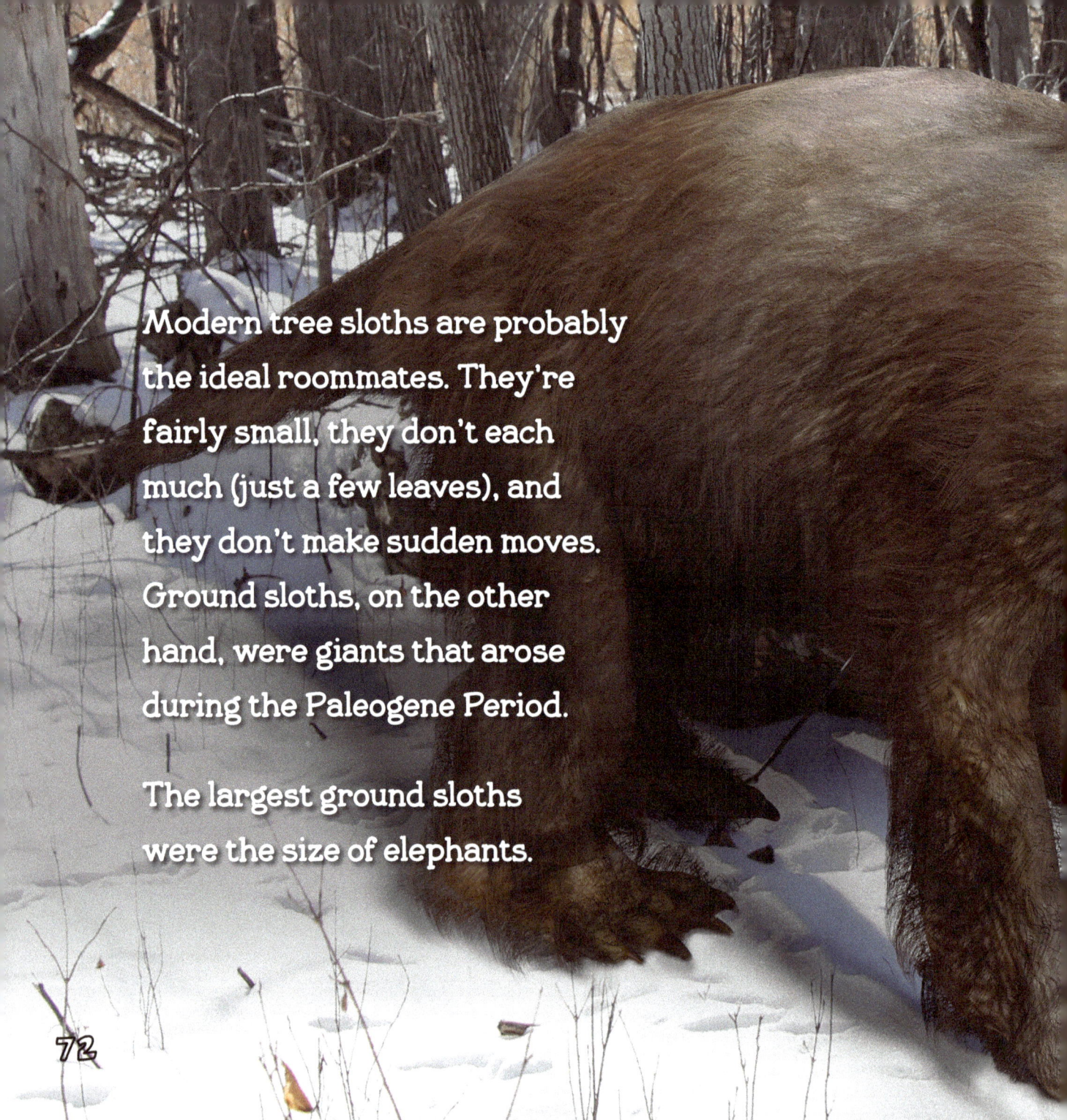

Modern tree sloths are probably the ideal roommates. They're fairly small, they don't each much (just a few leaves), and they don't make sudden moves. Ground sloths, on the other hand, were giants that arose during the Paleogene Period.

The largest ground sloths were the size of elephants.

They also dined on plant leaves, but probably ate hundreds of pounds or kilograms a day. (Get used to your fridge being full of salad.) AND, IF YOUR GROUND SLOTH ROOMIE ACCIDENTALLY SAT ON YOU, YOU'D BE SQUISHED!

WHO WOULD
WIN IN A FIGHT
BETWEEN A
SABER-TOOTHED
TIGER AND
A MODERN-DAY
TIGER?

DESPITE THEIR SIMILAR NAMES, THESE CATS ARE ONLY DISTANT COUSINS.

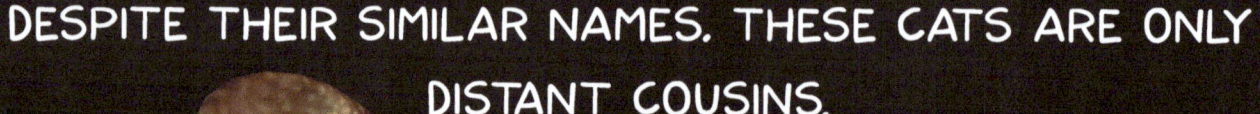

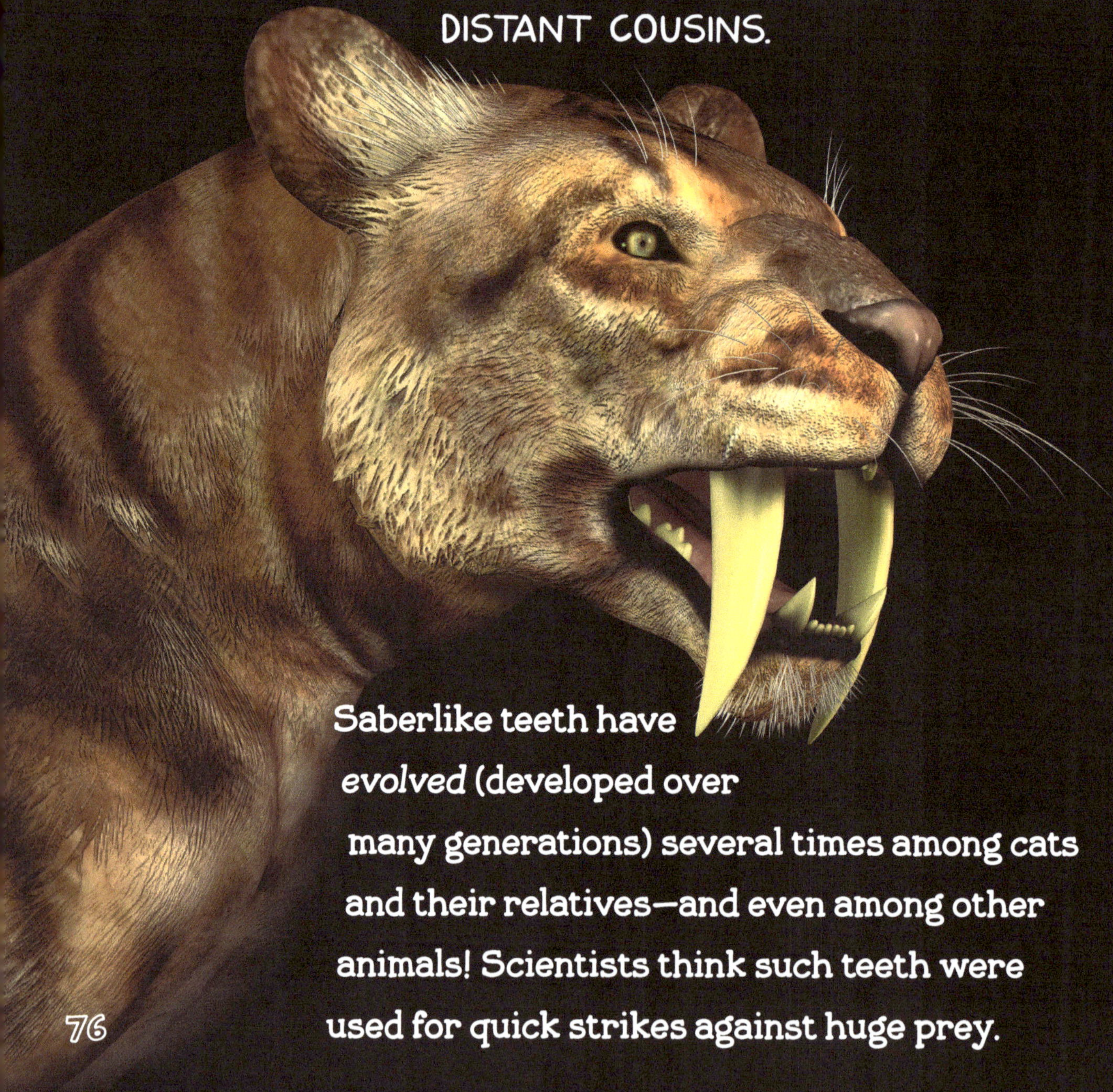

Saberlike teeth have *evolved* (developed over many generations) several times among cats and their relatives—and even among other animals! Scientists think such teeth were used for quick strikes against huge prey.

This strategy would fare poorly against a powerful, similar-sized predator like the modern tiger. The modern tiger might have the advantage.

WOULD YOU RATHER...

BE HUNTED BY A TYRANNOSAURUS

OR VELOCIRAPTORS?

Tyrannosaurus was a super predator with sharp eyes and a keen nose. It would be curtains for you if you fell into its sights—or scents.

Despite what you may have seen in movies, Velociraptor was only about 3 feet (1 meter) tall and 6 feet (2 meters) long from nose to tail.

AND, THERE'S NO SOLID EVIDENCE THAT THEY HUNTED IN PACKS!

WOULD YOU RATHER...

BUMP INTO A CREATURE

OR ONE CALLED AN

CALLED A LACE CRAB

UNUSUAL SHRIMP?

Anomalocaris, whose name means *unusual shrimp*, could grow up to 39 inches (100 centimeters) in length.

This fearsome animal was armed with grasping appendages and a circular mouth lined with bony plates.

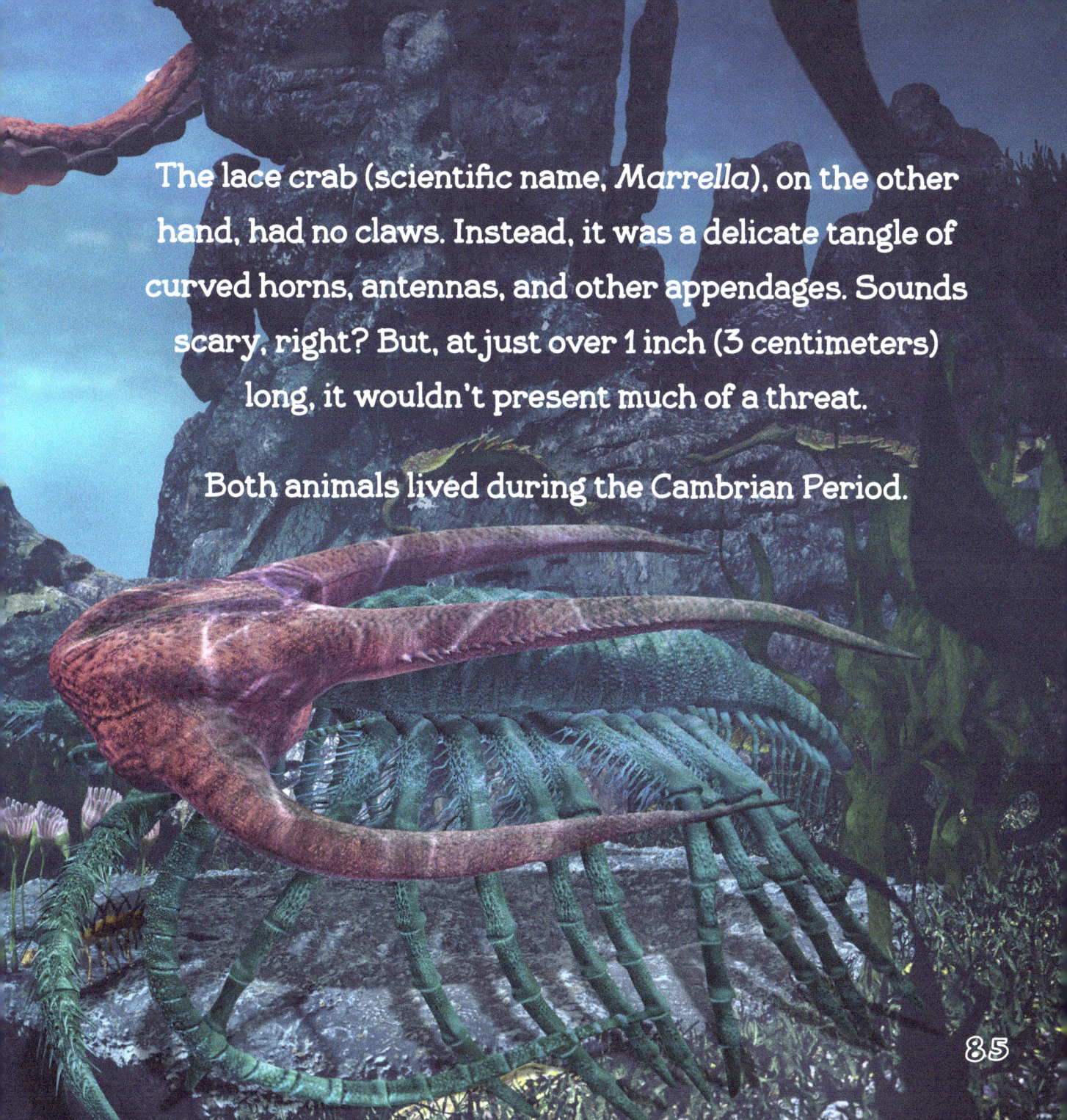

The lace crab (scientific name, *Marrella*), on the other hand, had no claws. Instead, it was a delicate tangle of curved horns, antennas, and other appendages. Sounds scary, right? But, at just over 1 inch (3 centimeters) long, it wouldn't present much of a threat.

Both animals lived during the Cambrian Period.

...CLIMB THE TALLEST TREE THAT EVER LIVED, OR THE NECK OF THE TALLEST DINOSAUR?

The Jurassic Period dinosaur *Brachiosaurus* was 40 feet (12 meters) tall. But it probably wouldn't appreciate you scaling its long neck.

The biggest trees of all time are still alive today! The tallest known redwood tree, in northern California, stands over 377 feet (115 meters) tall. Better pack a lunch: it's going to be a long climb.

WOULD YOU RATHER...

...live through the end-Cretaceous extinction, which killed off the dinosaurs, or the end-Permian extinction, known as the Great Dying?

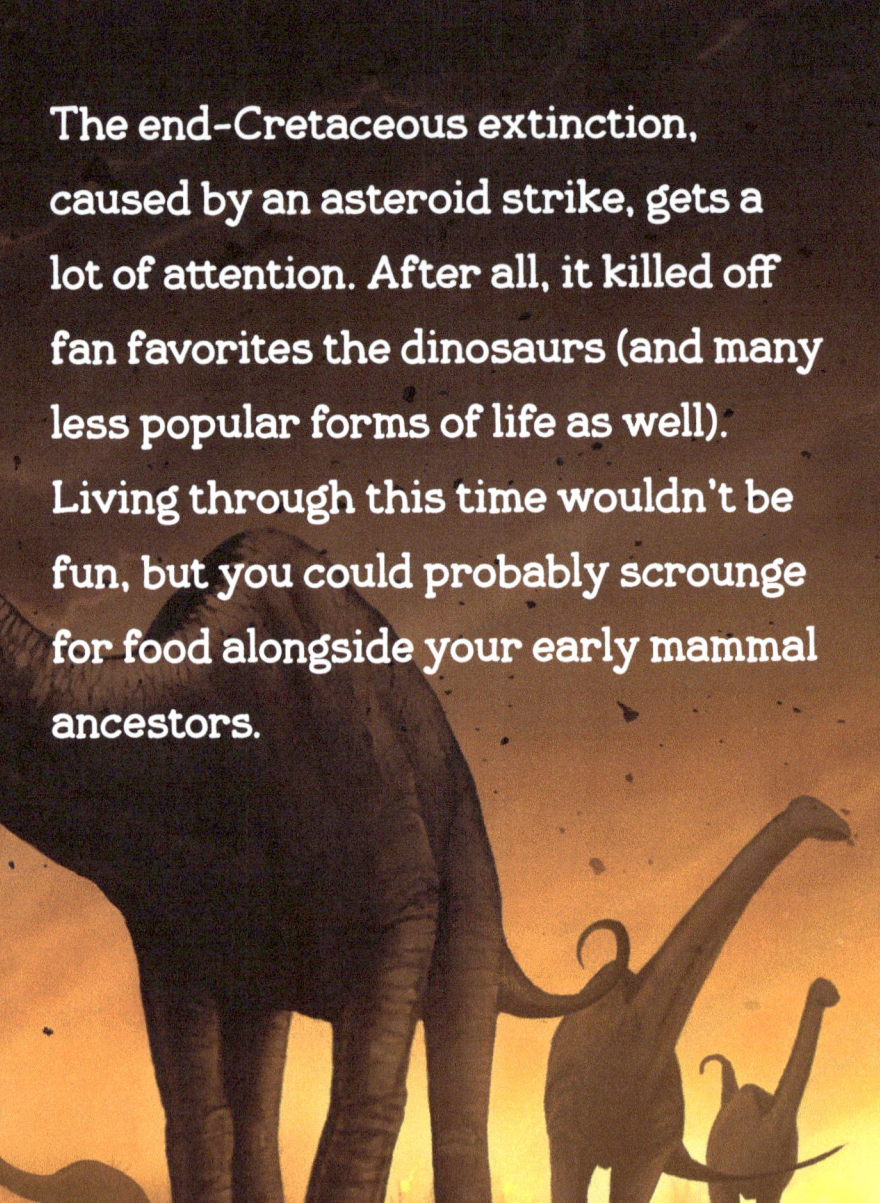

The end-Cretaceous extinction, caused by an asteroid strike, gets a lot of attention. After all, it killed off fan favorites the dinosaurs (and many less popular forms of life as well). Living through this time wouldn't be fun, but you could probably scrounge for food alongside your early mammal ancestors.

The end-Permian extinction, on the other hand, is called the Great Dying because multi-celled life was nearly wiped out. Scientists aren't sure what caused the extinction, but almost 95 percent of species disappeared. There'd be barely any food to scrounge.

ENGAGE YOUR READER

GUIDED READING PROMPTS

Before Reading
- Allow readers to scan the text and discuss what they notice so far. Highlight the structure of this text and discuss a plan for reading.
- Explain the literacy skill: *Everyone has opinions! Those opinions are based on reasons. As you read, think about the facts and reasoning that might persuade you to believe or choose a certain thing.*

During Reading
- Read each question and provide time to discuss the options as well as your readers' answers before turning the page to learn the facts. Did these facts persuade your readers to change their minds?
- As you read, model how to identify the facts, reasoning, and any counterarguments used in the text. Prompt your readers to identify these features as they explore the text, too!
- Practice the skills of retelling and summarizing by prompting your readers to rephrase the reasoning found in the text in their own words.

After Reading
- Explain to your readers that persuasive arguments can sometimes cause us to change our opinions: *Part of learning and growing involves gathering new information and using it to inform our thinking. Sometimes this can cause us to change our minds about something!*
- Have your readers reflect on a specific part of the text and complete the sentence frame: "I used to think _____, now I think _____ because…"

LOOK BACK!
- Prompt readers to look back through the text to identify examples of strong reasons that supported the persuasive arguments.
- Challenge your readers by asking them to identify examples of counterarguments and explain how they made the persuasive argument stronger.

COMMON CORE CONNECTIONS
These questions and tasks align with the following Common Core College and Career Readiness Anchor Standards for Reading:
- CCSS.ELA-Literacy.CCRA.R.1
- CCSS.ELA-Literacy.CCRA.R.4
- CCSS.ELA-Literacy.CCRA.R.5
- CCSS.ELA-Literacy.CCRA.R.8
- CCSS.ELA-Literacy.CCRA.R.10

LITERACY SKILL

To persuade means to convince someone to believe or do something. A persuasive argument includes all the reasons that might convince someone to believe or do that thing.

Strong persuasive arguments include:
- Topic: What are you trying to convince someone to believe or do?
- Audience: Who do you want to persuade?
- Reasons: What might convince this audience? Why should they believe or do what you want them to? Great reasons are supported by facts. Some reasons even include counterarguments to make them stronger.

Example from the text: Pages 10-13
- Topic: Who would win in a fight – *Tyrannosaurus rex* or *Spinosaurus,* the largest dinosaur predator known?
- Audience: Readers like you!
- Reasons: Despite *Spinosaurus* being about 10 feet (3 meters) longer than *Tyrannosaurus rex*, it likely would not have won in a fight. Some fossils suggest that *Spinosaurus* may have been partly aquatic, so its jaws would have been better at catching fish than battling creatures that lived on land. In addition, *Tyrannosaurus rex* had massive jaws that could cut through bone! It would likely be the winner in a battle.

EXTEND THROUGH WRITING

Ask your readers what they wonder about prehistoric animals.
- Have readers research prehistoric animals and make note of any wild, fun, or interesting facts related to them. Have readers look for connections or comparisons and ask themselves, "what can I ask about these facts that might evoke some strong opinions?"
- Direct readers to fold a piece of paper in half, write their question on the outside, and include their persuasive argument addressing that question on the inside.

MORE WAYS TO ENGAGE!
- Use the Would You Rather questions to practice accountable talk and respectful ways to engage in discussion.
- Add a little movement to your routine! Determine two places in the room, one for each Would You Rather answer option. Ask readers to stand and cross the room to the answer they would rather choose.
- Connect to mathematics by using the Would You Rather questions as a survey tool. Collect data and create bar graphs to analyze trends in responses.

World Book, Inc.
180 North LaSalle Street
Suite 900
Chicago, Illinois 60601
USA

Copyright © 2023 (print and e-book) World Book, Inc. All rights reserved.

This volume may not be reproduced in whole or in part in any form without prior written permission from the publisher.

WORLD BOOK and the GLOBE DEVICE are registered trademarks or trademarks of World Book, Inc.

For information about other "Would You Rather..." titles, as well as other World Book print and digital publications, please go to www.worldbook.com.

For information about other World Book publications, call 1-800-WORLDBK (967-5325).

For information about sales to schools and libraries, call 1-800-975-3250 (United States) or 1-800-837-5365 (Canada).

Library of Congress Cataloging-in-Publication Data for this volume has been applied for.

Would You Rather…
ISBN: 978-0-7166-4738-6 (set, hc.)

Would You Rather… Visit Disneyland or Jurassic Park?
…and other mammoth questions about prehistoric animals
ISBN: 978-0-7166-4746-1 (hc.)

Also available as:
ISBN: 978-0-7166-4756-0 (e-book)

Printed in India by Thomson Press (India) Limited,
Uttar Pradesh, India
1st printing June 2022

STAFF

Editorial

Writer
William D. Adams

Senior Manager, New Content
Jeff De La Rosa

Manager, New Product
Nick Kilzer

Curriculum Designer
Caroline Davidson

Proofreader
Nathaniel Lindstrom

Graphics and Design

Senior Designer
Brenda Tropinski

Freelance designers
Francis Paola Lea
Luciana Antonella Quintana Guerrero

Senior Media Editor
Rosalia Bledsoe

ACKNOWLEDGMENTS

Cover: © Wadha adnan/Shutterstock; © sruilk/Shutterstock; © Thomas Pajot, Shutterstock; © ItzaVU/Shutterstock; © metha1819/Shutterstock	34-37 © Roman Uchytel, Prehistoric Fauna
1-7 © Shutterstock	38-39 © Martin Shields, Alamy Images
8-9 © Stocktrek Images, Inc./Alamy Images	40-51 © Shutterstock
10-11 © Alfonso Fabio Iozzino, Alamy Images	52-53 © Genevieve Vallee, Alamy Images
12-13 © Imagebroker/Alamy Images; © Abduramanova Elena, Shutterstock	54-55 WORLD BOOK illustration by Francis Paola Lea
14-15 © dotted zebra/Alamy Images	56-57 © Peter Schickert, Alamy Images
16-17 © Stocktrek Images/SuperStock	58-59 © wave break media/Shutterstock
18-19 © Christian Thompson, Disneyland Resort; © sruilk/Shutterstock; © Thomas Pajot, Shutterstock; © ItzaVU/Shutterstock	60-61 © Roman Uchytel, Prehistoric Fauna
20-21 © Universal Pictures	62-71 © Shutterstock
22-29 © Shutterstock	72-73 © Roman Uchytel, Prehistoric Fauna
30-31 © J.A. Chirinos	74-75 © apiguide/Shutterstock
32-33 © Julio Lacerda, Studio 252MYA	76-77 © Corey Ford, iStockphoto; © Sukpaiboonwat/Shutterstock
	78-79 © Urban Zone/Alamy Images
	80-91 © Shutterstock
	92-93 © Mark Garlick, Science Source; © Julio Lacerda, Studio 252MYA
	94 © NeMaria/Shutterstock; © ShiipArt/Shutterstock

www.ingramcontent.com/pod-product-compliance
Lightning Source LLC
Chambersburg PA
CBHW060948170426
43201CB00023B/2418